Balancing Between

My Master &

My Mate

By

Dr. Veynell Warren

Table of Contents

Chapter 1 Balance Vs. Juggle..........7

Chapter 2 Deny My Selfish Ways....18

Chapter 3 Weigh the Cost 24

Chapter 4 From Fantasy to Dream To Reality............................30

Chapter 5 Private Worship..........40

Chapter 6 Family Worship..........45

Chapter 7 Marriage as Ministry.....51

Chapter 8 Provider as Mate.........60

Covenant Agreement Husband 66

Covenant Agreement Wife.... 67

Copyright © 2017 by Crazy Faith Publishing
P.O. Box 41639, Dallas, TX 75241
www.veynellwarren.com

Balancing Between My Master and My Mate by Dr. Veynell Warren

ISBN 978-1976418884 (Createspace)

All rights reserved. No part of this book may be reproduced, stored in a retrieval system, or transmitted in any form or by any means – electronic, mechanical, photocopy, recording, or any other—except for brief quotations in printed reviews, without the prior written consent of the publisher. If you purchase this book without a cover you should be aware that this book may have been stolen property and reported as "unsold and destroyed" to the Publisher. In such case neither the author nor the publisher has received any payment for this "stripped book."

Scripture quotations marked (KJV) are taken from the Holy Bible, Copyright © 1973, 1978, 1984 by Biblica, Inc. ™ Used by permission of Zondervan. All rights reserved worldwide. www.zondervan.com

Scripture quotations marked NKJV are taken from the New King James Version. Copyright 1982 Thomas, Nelson, Inc. Used by permission. All rights reserved.

Scripture quotations marked AMP are from The Amplified Bible, Old Testament copyright 1965, 1987 by the Zondervan Corporation. The Amplified Bible, New Testament copyright 1954, 1958, 1987 by The Lockman Foundation. Used by permission. All rights reserved.

Dedication

To God Almighty, His Son Jesus Christ and the Inspiring Holy Ghost

Special Thanks to

Masterful Collective

Grace Files, Daphanie Smith

Rhema Scent

Flamekeepers

Believer's International Ministries

Unique Attractions

More Precious Than This Photography

G.N.A. & I.N.A.

Lindart Collections

Apostle Demond L. Tolliver

Elise Shedd

Crazy Faith Entertainment

UA Network TV

Pam and Lee Sherrell

My beautiful daughters, Jesny and Vanequa Warren

My handsome sons, Wayne and Tyrell Warren

Introduction

The word marriage ignites many opposing emotions in people. Some may immediately dream everlasting love and eternal bliss. While others may consider marriage unnecessary because it's reduced to just a piece of paper. The desire for marriage is one of greatest pursuits for Christians today. Marriage is honorable, and it is a union destined by God. In my marital experience as a "successful failure" it allowed me the chance to evaluate my failures in my marriage and develop and refine the true principles both spiritual and natural essential to creating balance, a strong bond and true intimacy. Through my journey I have counseled countless couples for varying reasons, some needed to regain what was lost, others desired marriage for selfish reasons. Decide today to begin your life changing marital journey and discover how to balance between your master and your mate.

Chapter 1 Balance Vs Juggle

In my experience I found that there are foundational characteristics necessary to be a true balanced husband or wife in a marriage ordained by God. Both spouses must possess the godly characteristics. One thing that any man or woman must deny is their fleshly desires to become unified in holy matrimony. People assume that because you are godly doesn't mean you don't have temptations in the flesh. A method to implore to not be imbalanced in marriage is to get your flesh in check. There's a balance between God and self that must align with the Holy Ghost to keep the flesh in check. The first thing you must master before your mate comes along is the desires for the things of your flesh and the world. In 1 John 2:15-17 God instructs us to not love the world neither what's in the world. That includes the lust of the flesh, and the lust of the eyes and the pride of life. For whatever you are before you get married is what you're going to bring to the marriage. Mastering your flesh takes submitting one's will and life completely to God. You still should keep the flesh in control even when you get married. People struggle and juggle in marriage because they never laid their carnal and selfish desires at the altar. The gift of marriage is a union with one man to one woman for ministry and pursing Kingdom work in the earth. Marriage is more than permission to enjoy unlimited sexual intercourse and companionship. You must deny yourself to meet the needs of someone else on a continual basis until death do you part. It is imperative for both men and women to relinquish singular characteristics before marriage. These characteristics are being selfish, self-centered or lustful. Ensure you aren't dipping and dabbling in sin while expecting God to bless you with a mate. Otherwise you're going to be juggling sin and commitment which is like oil and water which can't mix cohesively but naturally separate. There should be a balance of God, holiness and consecration before you enter the sanctity of marriage. The flesh can recall and remember what it has experienced. Be conscience not to bring lustfulness, freaky tendencies and carnal desires into marriage and expect it to be productive and fulfilling. Perversion is one thing that can defile the marriage bed especially if both spouses were still participating in those types of activities before they got married. It's more than just fornicating and committing sexual sin but it's the soul ties, spirit and sharing bondage within the marriage. That's why it's not good to touch a man or woman because it causes the flesh to speak louder than the spirit of God. Once the flesh has experienced fleshly pleasure, there becomes an instant appetite to satisfy the flesh along with a continual battle to subdue the sexual desires. If you were a flirt, whoremonger, a cheater, an adulterer, or fornicator for one or both sexes, then you must make sure that no residue of those spirits are in you and that they have completely died spiritually. The Greatest Enemy to a godly marriage is not just the devil alone but the enemy created by choices from within. We alone can sabotage our own lives and other people because of our selfish tendencies and ways. Marriage is a covenant union between a man and woman created by God and is an earthly representation of God's relationship with His people. Self must die and become one with another person to be fulfilled and accomplish greater works in the Kingdom of God on the earth. God desires for His people to become one with His Spirit, subject to His power and fully accepting His love so we can truly live in balance in our spiritual and natural walk in this life. The marital union is rich and full of more than just getting with someone, so you can have companionship in your life, have children and be fully satisfied. As the vows declare marriage should not be entered into lightly because ultimately, it's a spiritual cord that will affect generations to come. God called His people His Bride because we are in a divine covenant with God and work with God to fulfill what He desires to do for mankind in the earth. Our flesh constantly fights to stay on one accord with God. God is like a patient husband, with grace He loves us despite our wrong doings, continual mistakes and constant struggles because He is married to the backslider. This is where the juggling happens when we try to please our flesh instead of God and wonder how we can please our spouse if we can't please God. Everything that happens in marriage is symbolic on how God's people act and treat God sometimes committing adultery and seeking other lovers to please themselves. Adultery in marriage has the same affect because we are betraying our union with another person by seeking other lovers outside of the union. If we are so easy to break covenant with God, how are we going to maintain a covenant with another human being for a lifetime? If any part of "self" is hindering your spiritual walk with God, it's going to hinder the marriage as well. When there's an imbalance between unity with God because of self then it's hard to truly become one with another person. Denying oneself is more than just the flesh but putting our desires down to work together with someone else to complete a greater cause in the earth. Marriage is the ultimate sacrifice of self and denying self daily because now you and your spouse have become one. There's no I or me but we in the relationship. Let's look deeply at the sacrifice of Isaac and Abraham in its meaning to deny self and giving up what we truly and really love even when it's a promise from God. You will not be able to truly love someone fully until you give up what you desire or want the most. What you are willing to give up determines how much God can entrust and endow you with. When denying self is mastered then the Spirit of the Lord governs your actions, then marriage truly begins to be what God created it to be where there's oneness in mind, body, soul and spirit. The next step of progressing and transitioning into marriage is self-sacrifice. In Genesis 22, Abraham had finally received what God had promised Him which was his son, Isaac. Well, God tested Abraham's love for Him by offering his son Isaac as a living sacrifice high on a mountain. Abraham, being obedient to

God, prepared to sacrifice his only son, he built an altar unto the Lord to give him up as a burnt offering. When God saw that Abraham was willing to give up what he loved the most to please God he was richly blessed by God (Genesis 22:1-17). Marriage takes giving up what we love the most to please one another and agree in every decision and action that we make. To reach a place of experiencing a blessed marriage, you must sacrifice everything you love the most to create a sustaining atmosphere for a fulfilled marriage. If you search your heart and ask the difficult question: What is it that I love the most? The result of loving something more than your spouse can result in a hinderance. The hinderance can be you not fully submitting to your spouse in marriage or your affections being focused in other places. Marriages can dissolve because of self-destructive behavior and they weren't ready to give up themselves to make the marriage work. You have to offer yourself up to God to be prepared for marriage and allow Him to purify you by fire and tests to walk in the blessed state of marriage. So many people desire to be married but are they truly and totally prepared for this next phase in their spiritual and natural life. Marriage is an elevation or promotion of ones' single status to the next dimension, power and glory of God in the earth. Our single state is the time where we are becoming one with God, denying our self and allowing God to create us into what He designed us to be from the beginning of the world. Marriage is not just a natural progression to living the good life and having the wood picket fence, the house and the children. Marriage wasn't created just for sex, socioeconomic status and security but to glorify God in the earth. The life of married people is a balance of God and spouse which only works when both man and woman are on one accord in spirit, mind and body. In 1 Corinthians 7:32-34, Apostle Paul addressed unmarried men and women describing the balance they must have in serving God and pleasing our spouse. But one must master the single state of caring for the things of God before they can transition into the married state. Men who are married care for the things of the world which is pleasing his wife and "his interests are divided" (AMP). The same thing goes for the woman. Divided means an equal balance of mastering serving God and pleasing your mate. That only happens when you and your mate are on one accord and not unequally yoked. The scripture that everyone uses to not choose the wrong mate found in 2 Corinthians 5:11, is more than just yoking or connecting with an unbeliever. You and your mate can both be Christians in God but one may walk in unbelief in some areas of their spiritual walk. One mate may still possess selfish tendencies and not as selfless as the other causing a spiritual juggle of in the area of meeting one another's needs. One may take their assignment in God more serious than the other while the other one still walks in their flesh in areas of their life. One likes to pray and fast more than the other one who only does it when he or she feels like it. It will be a constant juggle and struggle in your marriage if you are yoked unequally which hinders unity and growth. Imbalance in marriages causes divisions and allows for a breach to occur allowing Satan an opportunity to enter to destroy the marriage from within. You and your mate must serve only one master which is God. While you are single, what other masters, idols or things are still hindering or blocking you totally allowing God to be the Master over your life? You cannot serve two masters and a mate (Matthew 6:24 KJV). A man can't serve his flesh, God and a mate because it blocks unity. In Matthew 19:5-6, A man leaves all to join his wife in marriage becoming one flesh (KJV). When God puts two people together in the unity of marriage, the Master and Mate become one. As God cleaves to His People, they become one with His Spirit and Glory. That is why divorce was never part of God's plan for marriage because it represents a broken divine covenant. God hates when covenants are broken from His people and marriage. Marriage shouldn't never be taken lightly or without counsel because God takes it very seriously. There must be balance in serving God and your mate meaning you can't spend more time in ministry and neglect your spouse. You must devote equal time to God and your mate. Your mate is a gift from God that wishes to be treasured, nurtured and protected. One practice that will assist in an imbalance and avoid the juggling of Master and Mate is to be intentional about scheduling time with your Mate especially for those in full-time ministry. These practical steps are a healthy balance that ensures God is glorified. It is equally important that you cultivate the needs of your mate with quality time, attention and satisfying desires. God expects us to honor Him through how we care and treat our mate He has gifted to us.

Chapter 2
Deny My Selfish Ways

Self must be dealt with and submitted to God's will completely. Submission in God's perspective is allowing yourself to agree with someone for the greater good or cause of continuing the pursuit of being one. In the single state, man or woman must first submit to God concerning their will which means to totally surrender oneself to the full plan of God in one's life. What's the full plan of God? People think that doing the will of God means they have surrender to God completely which isn't always the case. Our selfish flesh nature doesn't naturally desire the things of the spirit but to align your flesh with God's will we will have to give up all of our fleshly desires and ways. Yes, we can serve God but choose to compartmentalize how we serve Him and what part of His will we do for ourselves. Yet, if you look at it when we are not fully obedient and aligned to God's perfect will, spiritual and natural imbalance is inevitable. You can't serve God and mammon (Matthew 6:24 KJV). Mammon is more than money and can be anything that is warring with your total submission to God's will. You can't partially submit to God and fully reach the ultimate place in God. You can be gifted, anointed, and used greatly by God but if you're still trying to please or serve those aspects of your life that serve as mammon, you will always be in conflict and at war with yourself. Now in terms of marriage, you can't serve and please yourself and not think about pleasing your soulmate. It would be a difficult place to be in as you consider excellence in serving God and your selfish tendencies. Be decisive in choosing to love God and hate your fleshly desires, your spoiled nature, or your selfish ways. We naturally desire to please the flesh on one hand but hate when God convicts you and you must repent for your selfish acts. The spirit of compromise occurs when we are trying to serve two masters and haven't truly submitted to the whole plan of God in our lives.

God's plan will yield His peace and rest. Rest is more than just going to sleep but when we will align to God's will and choose not to submit to two masters anymore. You won't have a successful marriage if you have self-seeking tendencies and disregard the needs and wants of your spouse. Submission in God helps our spirit and soul be at rest leaving little room for anxiety, fears, frustrations, anger, and self-centeredness. The single state of a person must be maximized to the point that our soul is at rest in God and we are in total submission and ready to submit to another in unity. Total submission will result in total satisfaction. Disunity in marriages occur because of restless souls trying to unify in marriage but still are divided by outside influences. To be able to serve God and your spouse, self must be submitted to God and self must please your spouse as it pleases God. Marriage is a covenant agreement to unconditionally submit to one another because they are totally submitted to God. In Hebrews 4:1-11, God speaks on those who find rest in Him for those that believe in Him and trust to follow His Word completely (KJV). Those who are not in God's rest may struggle with unbelief and still walk in some areas of disobedience which is why they are not at rest in God nor at peace. The Word of God cuts and dissects the soul of man and exposes our true heart. That exposed, naked and broken heart will be seen and even handled by your spouse. The Holy Spirit helps us to submit our true selves to the work of God to mold and shape us in our divine image sculpted by God before the foundation of the world. God's image isn't selfish nor self-seeking but giving, loving, and submissive to the Word of God. Even God is totally submitted to His Word and keeps His Word. God displayed how unselfish He was by sacrificing His only son Jesus to save mankind from damnation. Even Jesus had to submit His will to His Father even when his flesh didn't want to partake in the cup of suffering. If we can't totally commit to God, then how can we totally submit to another person? God wants us to let go of ourselves and be a masterpiece. That means our old habits and selfish ways must be crucified at the altar for God to truly take us to that new place in Him. Carnal Christians live out more of their flesh rather than the leading of the Spirit. This selfishness leads disobedience to God's will. When you're not carnal and want to serve God, but don't want to give up the very thing you love to receive everything God has for you can lead to the same disobedience in serving the flesh. What you truly love the most besides God and even your spouse will always be a hindrance in your marriage. Your spouse will always come in second to what you love the most. If you enter marriage with a selfish mindset at all cost you get what you want even if it supersedes what your spouse wants or needs, this is going to cause a spiritual seesaw effect. You and your spouse will both be going up and down on getting what you want instead of being submitted to one another to mutually get what each one desires. In Ephesians 5:21-31, the scripture discusses how marriage is to biblically function in terms of submission and two becoming one flesh. It doesn't say one submit and the other remain selfish, but both submit to one another. Wives must learn how to submit to God and make Him head over their lives to be in a position to do the same for their husband. If she's not submitted and committed to God wholeheartedly, she will display the same behavior with her husband. The husband is not exempt, if he doesn't learn to love God and give himself to God's will in His life, then he will do likewise when he gets married. The scriptures speak on both spouses being submitted to God and each other. This spiritual balance leads to the oneness process in Ephesians 5:29-31 in which the man loves the wife as he loves himself. Selfish ways block this oneness in marriage. When he is married, his wife becomes connected to him spiritually and physically. Spouses will cherish one another when they deny the appetites of the flesh and come together in the union of marriage which is a covenant agreement. Then they can serve God and please their spouse with long lasting joy and true fulfillment.

Chapter 3 Weigh the Cost

The lifestyle of marriage requires commitment, sacrifices, and loyalty. The unseen costs involved in marriage is more than the wedding, the honeymoon and the ring solely. There are spiritual investments if you decide to marry the right or wrong person. God doesn't transition us into the marriage state if He knows we are not ready to pay the cost of marriage and value the importance of it. People think they are ready for marriage because the physical and tangible aspects of life are abundant. However, the spiritual side is equally important and that will be proven as the marriage progresses over time. The vows of a wedding are sequential in describing marriage professing to endure, hold on to, for better or worse, for richer or poorer, in sickness and in health until death do us part. This is the price of marriage, are you willing to pay? We must weigh the cost of what it takes to have a successful marriage and understand that it is a vow we are saying before God that establishes the covenant. In the Bible, vows are serious matters with God and He takes them as a promise that He intends for you to keep. A vow is a promise or oath to do a specific thing. When a man and woman stand before a minister to say their vows, God hears these vows and hold them accountable to them. God takes marriage very seriously and nowadays divorces can cost more than the marriage. In Ecclesiastes 5:5, the scripture says that, "Better is it that thou shouldest not vow, than thou shouldest vow and not pay." Vows are to be honored and paid in God's eyes so when people don't weigh the cost when it comes to entering marriage, it's inevitable that challenges will occur. When we take vows before God concerning marriage, there's a spiritual connection that happens unseen by the flesh but seen by God that authorizes the blessing or the curses to flow in the couple's life. As a couple takes the vow especially in marriage, they are providing a covenant oath to devote themselves to each other that can only be broken by a natural or spiritual death. Whatever or whoever you vow to connect to can either hinder or push your spiritual walk with God. This can take place gradually. The spiritual connection of marriage is also recognized by the devil and his demonic army whether you belong with that person or not. Vows seal the deal or fate of your marriage. Accountability increases in the union because you have joined your soul with another soul developing positive or negative soul ties. Unequally yoked people in marriage develop what we call "legal soul ties" and call it being married. The ultimate cost of marriage is the state of your soul. Who you join yourself to in terms of marriage can either complement or cause agony to your soul. The condition of your soul weighs more than a house, a grand wedding, a honeymoon and having children. Souls are meant to connect divinely with other people for divine purposes not just fleshly pleasures. Coming together as a couple is more than just sex. In God's perfect will towards our life He predestined who we are to marry before birth. Therefore, we don't need to sample the goods or product through sexual fornication prematurely. Sexual intimacy was designed by God as a benefit to those who entered the covenant of marriage. It wasn't created for just pleasing one another. Some people don't weigh the cost of marriage and just want to have sex, procreate and enjoy sexual satisfaction with each other which is why some hasten to be married. The scripture in 1 Corinthians 7:9 where Paul discusses that "It's better to marry than to burn," describes if the couple can't control their urges they should get married. When a marriage is based on the burn and passion of sex there will be challenges that a couple didn't prepare for because they compromised placing the flesh before the spirit. Marriage isn't solely designed solely for permission to have unlimited sex. In our single state, we must keep a level of consecration and sanctification before marriage even occurs. When two bodies become one flesh in marriage, that means flesh has been crucified and prepared spiritually for the oneness in marriage. It is better to marry instead of burning with lust is to not tempt your flesh in compromising situations through premarital sex, fornication and other sexual activities outside the order of God. This does not mean that you have the free liberty and license to marry somebody so you can have all the sex you want. Also, marriage doesn't give you legal access to let your inhibitions go and embark in perverted activities. The spirit of perversion runs rampant in marriages which is why it's important to know a person's sexual proclivities and past. Knowing a person's sexual history is important and even more so to avoid contracting a sexually transmitted disease because of your spouse not being truthful. People behind closed doors can be an inward pervert and a person may experience a vexation of their soul because they are married to a perverted person who wants to participate in perverted activities. It's worse when your perverted spouse wants you to be intimate with them and you have no desire to participate in any twisted activities that cause violent pain or humiliation, such as orgies, multiple partners at once, switching partners or sadomasochism. You must weigh the cost of your soul as more important than just marrying someone because they are nice and go to church. Seek God in prayer to show you areas of concern or secret sins that will come out surprisingly in your married life. Being married doesn't mean you are free from temptation and things coming your way to appease your flesh. You still have a responsibility to keep your flesh subject to the Holy Spirit so that you and your spouse are equipped to live a holy and consecrated life. Your eyes must be watchful for serpents, snakes, and wolves that come in the guise of church clothes, suits, and hats. To maintain the strength of your marriage, prayer and fasting is the key to outweighing the attacks, warfare, and challenges that will come against you and your spouse.

Chapter 4 From Fantasy to Dream to Reality

People have made the wedding day seem like the only important component that occurs when two people get married. TV shows, books, movies and stores sell the illusion of wedded bliss and happy matrimony on the day the bride and groom say, 'I do'. Women flock to bridal stores, cutting out dream wedding gowns and making scrapbooks even setting a table for two. They have endless fantasies about how they want their dream wedding. The dress, the ceremony, the ring and the fairy tale of marriage is sold to every woman who believes that one day their prince will come and sweep them away. Once the day of nuptials happens, it's now happily ever after and the couple now can live the life of true fulfillment and happiness in marriage. But the women aren't the only ones that deal with fantasies and high expectations about their mate being this knight and shining armor who loves the Lord, a mighty man of

God who preaches and he is anointed as well. Men also have a fantasy and preconceived notion about how perfect the church lady should be. The perfect church lady is the desired role of any woman in the church desiring to be married to a man of the cloth. The pastor's wife is the ideal mate for some men who want a church wife who can sing, preach, speak in tongues, lay hands and pray for others and quite beautiful. Women join churches hoping to become the First Lady or Elect Lady thinking that their soulmate is a man in the church including the one overseeing the church. Being known as the pastor's wife has the same importance and clout as a woman being married to the Prince of England. A holy preaching man desires for his wife to be a Proverbs 31 woman anointed to hear from God, beautiful and fashionable dressed. A woman who is faithful to God is very attractive to a godly man. Often times in the church there is a fantasy belief that those who are popular have a greater chance of marrying a prominent man or woman of God in the gospel. Also, seeking a mate has become more like a hunting game rather than an opportunity to fellowship and hear from the Lord and pray about the person. People come to church with an outward appearance of perfection which can translate into you automatically assume they are holy and righteousness. Men and women wear their Sunday's best so they can catch the eye of the right mate. Church services have become more like club services where both sexes strut their stuff while all eyes are on them. Physical attraction is good at first to catch the eye of a man or woman. After the first impression it's important to determine if they have a personal relationship with God. Ask yourself if they praise God, pray openly, shout, worship and serve in ministry. If they pray with some authority, then you got the right mate on this one. A scripture used repeatedly on the order of courtship and marriage found in Proverbs 18:22 says, "He who finds a wife finds a good thing and obtain favor from the Lord" (NKJV). Preachers preach this scripture to let men and women know that the man is supposed to find the wife and the woman needs to be hidden until her mate finds her. In the book of Ruth in the bible, Boaz found Ruth working in the vineyard. While women's rights have poised women to believe they can find their mate, on the contrary godly women will be found by their husband. Christian women should refrain from pursuing men in courtship and marriage. When the man finds a suitable mate that God has approved by confirmation and he marries her then he receives great favor with the Lord. Even in the beginning of creation, in the book of Genesis, God created Eve for Adam for them to enjoy life on earth, be fruitful and multiply. Even then, marriage was designed to be pleasurable, fulfilling, and enjoyable for God's creation. God took a rib out of Adam's body to form a suitable mate. The ministry of marriage began with Adam and Eve living a blissful life in the Garden of Eden. They were living fulfilling lives with the earth to enjoy as long as they remained obedient and submissive to God. Yet even in the first marriage, reality began to set in when Adam and Eve's relationship was tested by external attacks and temptations. It was pleasant and heavenly until sin and disobedience entered the garden. Adam did not protect his wife like he should with prayer and watching out for the enemy who comes unsuspecting and suddenly. Eve had gotten away from her spiritual covering being lured by a seducing spirit. When both spouses aren't watching out for the enemy or allow the enemy access through an open door, that's when problems in the marriage can begin. Why was the serpent able to infiltrate the first marriage? Through a selfish desire for the forbidden. The forbidden represents anything that God warns us that isn't good to do or have but it makes a person desire to have it even more so. The ideal of marriage can render unrealistic expectations and a misconception on how your soulmate is supposed to be. People get married and tend to create this unexpected fantasy that their soulmate is going to be a perfect person and now their lives are complete because he or she has a soulmate. Soulmates aren't perfect people and we can never expect for anyone to be perfect in every part of their life. A familiar myth is that there is this magical person called your soulmate that you have been connected to this soul before you both were born. It is just a matter of time until you both cross paths and meet one another fulfilling the destiny to marry and the melodious music plays in the background of the movie of your perfect life. Until reality kicks in and that soulmate isn't as perfect and magical as you perceive. Of course, when your soulmate disappoints you because they weren't what we thought they would or should be so we become dissatisfied with feelings of unfulfillment. That's when we begin to look for other options or alternatives to find fulfillment or satisfaction in our married life. God told Adam and Eve to not touch the tree because it would expose them to the forbidden and corrupt things of the world. By doing this simple act, it would corrupt their human nature to become easily dissatisfied, desiring fleshly things and pleasures that are forbidden or an abomination to God. Married people must make sure that they do not enter the forbidden areas in their flesh in which they begin to desire to do abominable things. When Eve tasted the fruit, her eyes became opened to the forbidden and she wanted her husband to partake of this act of pleasing the flesh. Pleasing the flesh began when Eve wanted something and got it through the act of disobedience. By eating the fruit, they opened the door to sin entering the world and mankind including a natural death. The wages of sin now became death spiritually and naturally for mankind, dooming us to eternal damnation. It took an incorruptible seed which was Jesus to restore the corrupt seed of mankind and destroy the works of the enemy against mankind. Beseeching the forbidden opens the doors to demonic invasion in one's life. Both Adam and Eve were now aware and exposed to knowing good and evil, so they now can choose between the two. Now their corrupt desire to do evil and carnal things to delight it. As a married couple, the bed must remain undefiled meaning not be exposed to perversion or the forbidden areas of perverted sex and seediness. When regular intimacy with your spouse isn't enough or becomes boring, then sometimes we think that going into the forbidden areas will make it more exciting and tantalizing. Being adventurous as a married couple is good but make sure that it doesn't open doors for other spirits to invade your marriage such as perversion. Satan uses disorder, chaos and confusion to cause a marriage to become unfulfilling and dissatisfied to both spouses. This can tempt spouses to seek other indulgences to satisfy their needs which can range from alcohol, drug use, adultery, swapping spouses and sexual perversion. A married couple, if they are not careful, can indulge and enter a place where they are fulfilling the lusts of their flesh for intimacy, power or to hide loneliness. People also use marriage for social promotion and to become what they call, the power couple. The pursuit for power can sometimes become part of why people get married thinking that they have a better chance for success having a person at their side. Therefore, people hope and pray that God send them a mate who is deemed as high profile, highly respected by their peers and very well connected. This ideal profile will ultimately provide the ultimate way of life. Even Christian people marry for power and success especially when it comes to advancing their names in the Body of Christ. Some churches were built on marriages based on selfish gain and desire for power, prestige and wealth. People try to marry people of their own kind based on their assignment to develop some spiritual connection and union, so they can build churches, get members, and get wealth using the guise of ministry and Kingdom work. However, it can be surprising what can occur behind closed doors of luxury living and expensive cars. Shockingly, drug use, alcohol abuse, domestic violence, sexual bondage and unhappiness for the couple who appear perfect on the exterior. It's not worth anyone's soul or life to marry and damn your soul to hell because of believing the marriage fantasy and not living the God kind of marriage. God's marriage is based on love for God and one another for the purpose of giving God glory, working together in ministry and doing Kingdom work. Marriage with purpose isn't defined by community work, traveling abroad doing missionary service, building multiple churches, or community centers, saving souls and helping the less fortunate. Yet, marriage is defined by the couple becoming one, serving each other as God gets the glory.

Chapter 5 Private Worship

Private worship time can become a greater challenge once you are married, so it is important to have it while you are single. Couples propose that they will spend more time with God once they get married and have equal private worship time with God as if they were single. Your marriage is supposed to enhance or accelerate your relationship with God not make it both individually and corporately as a unit. Your spouse is not to be the one to complete your spiritual walk with God nor fill in the gaps in your relationship with God. People have this misconception that to have wholeness and completion, you must seek and find it in another human being. Let's look at the misconception of completion and wholeness that comes from your soulmate rather than God. God did not create a spouse or soulmate to replace your relationship with Him but to enrich your love for Him. The love of God should be the first relationship we nurture and cultivate through intimacy with God through prayer, praise, and worship. God should be number one and lordship over your life especially as a single person. God's word says in Exodus 20:3 that "You shall have no other gods before me," meaning exactly what it says that nothing should be greater or become greater than your love and relationship with God. Otherwise that person is operating in a spirit of idolatry which is worshipping and seeking after everything else besides God. Putting things, people and situations before God and making them more of a high priority than maintaining a strong relationship with the Lord is idol worship. The world has given single people this deceptive notion that they are not complete or whole until they get married. People search for a soulmate to fill in that void that only God can fill. No human being can be your everything and it's unfair to develop an expectation that another person will make you whole and complete. People are flawed and imperfect. You can't expect another imperfect person to do what only God can do. God is supposed to be our everything in our single state before we think about marriage. Being single is the perfect time to become whole and complete in God not lacking or wanting nothing (James 1:4 KJV). We can't allow seeking a mate or the desire to get married to become an obsessive focus which can result in it becoming more important than seeking God. God wants to complete the work in your heart and mind before He allows you to be found (for women) and for you to find your wife (for men). Marriage or the ideal of marriage can become a form of idolatry in which we pursue finding of a mate with desperation hoping our relationship with God will get better once we get married. In the book of James 1:4, it says, "Let patience have its perfect work, that ye may be perfect and entire, wanting nothing." (KJV). Single people must allow God to perfect everything in their single status before they are ready to receive the manifestation of the promises of God. Marriage is His gift to you. Our relationship with God must be mastered and firmly solidified before we even get engaged to be married. Your private worship with God is going to determine how you love and treat your future spouse. Your love walk with God must be perfected to take on another human being and love them unconditionally. The love of God is the key to sustain and strengthen your marriage when attacks, trials and warfare come your way. To have the God kind of love is to be able to forgive and overcome mistakes, problems and struggles your spouse may have. Even in your private time with God, He must remain number one and center of your life as a married person. You can't serve God part-time while you are single and expect to reap the fullness of His blessings and promises in your life. God's promises including a mate is 2 Corinthians 1:20 reminds us, "For all the promises of God in Him are yea, and in Him Amen, unto the glory of God by us." (KJV) Yet the promises of God have conditions which are based on obedience and being fully committed to God's perfect will for our lives. If God knows you haven't totally surrendered your life to Him, He's not going bless you with a soulmate because he or she will become your god. God must be the one you can trust and rely on even when you are in a married state. It will be a priority to have private time with God which will strengthen your marriage and keep you prayed up against any attacks from the enemy. You and your spouse should have your own personal time that you two spend with God on a regular and consistent basis. Since the enemy despises marriages and unity, he works even harder to attack and try to bring wedges between you both so having a consistent prayer life is vital to the longevity of your marriage. Having a strong and personal relationship with God will produce a strong, fortified marriage that can withstand the attacks and fiery darts of the enemy. No one should every rely on their spouse for complete strength and power to weather every attack, trial, problem and demonic scheme. No man, woman, or spouse should ever take the place of God in your life.

Chapter 6 Family Worship

As man and wife, the union not only demands private worship but family worship with one another. There's power in unity of people especially those in covenant relationships like marriage. Satan is aware of this strength, so he persistently tries to bring division in the marriage. Division in a marriage can affect both persons and divide them mentally, physically, spiritually and emotionally. Both spouses must be on one accord to fight the schemes, devices and tactics of the enemy. The old saying, "A family that prays together, stays together," is relevant in keeping marriages together in peace and harmony. The scripture in Mark 10:9 that reads, "What therefore God hath joined together, let not man put asunder," (KJV) which means not allowing anyone or anything to cause discord or division in a relationship whether it is family, ministry or marriage. It's important to spend worship time with your spouse in prayer and fasting. Before you both say those covenant words I Do at the alter. During your engagement you should have the conversation and expectation of time for private and family worship. When the enemy comes to attack, he comes to destroy marriages and families because of the power of agreement. The power of agreement is the supernatural power of God that works with more than one individual to produce supernatural fruit because of the couple being on one accord and unity. God moves mightily in unity and this power of agreement is strengthened in the marriage when both spouses are on one accord spiritually. Developing a rhythm to intentionally spend family worship will reinforce the couple with spiritual cords that can withstand spiritual warfare. The husband is the head and spiritual leader of the household in the divine order of God. When the husband is the spiritual leader of the house, he must govern, guide, and lead his family to a deeper relationship with God and to serve the Lord wholeheartedly without compromise. The wife should follow the leading of her husband if he continues to follow the Lord. The spiritual leader of the family must lead the family to stay in the purposed will of God. He will also make corrections or adjustments to realign when necessary to prevent the Devil from invading or infiltrating the household. The husband and wife must keep in constant and open communication with God and each other to keep the marriage unified and fortified from attacks. Building and strengthening the walls of marriage requires, private and public worship that includes continuous prayer and identifying what I call," The Saboteurs of Marriage." One thing that sabotages any marriages quickly is if it wasn't sanctioned or ordained by God. If the marriage wasn't God ordained, then it's harder to withstand the attacks or weather the warfare that comes to the marriage. Division can set in quickly bringing a greater wedge between two people who were never supposed to unify which is why they have not become one in the spirit. Many of these marriages conclude in divorce especially if they are not spiritually strong or aware of Satan's devices. The goal of married couples joined together by God is to be aware of the traps and ditches the enemy uses to entrap them through the spirit of sabotage and division. The Saboteurs of Marriage can mask deception be any outside influences, bad associations, discord, family members, friends, and even co-laborer's in the Lord can destroy a good marriage if one is not watchful through negativity, criticism, and ungodly advice. Your family worship with your spouse is the time to voice your concerns and cover one another's faults or struggles in prayers. Reverence your spouse using discretion knowing what is said in your marriage should stay in your marriage. It should not be discussed with any outside sources including family unless it's a spiritual father or mother that may offer wisdom on the matter but always get permission from one another before uncovering your spouse. You still need to get each other's permission to reveal any marital issues to another person. During your private time with God, He helps perfect the things that concerns you in your marriage and continuing to intercede for your spouse will reap its rewards in the future. Bad associations and connections with other people can bring wedges in a marriage. The wrong influences and connections can lead marriages to their demise and doom especially if these connections harbor any jealousy, resentment or malice towards you and your spouse. You can't hang around or talk with everyone because people carry spirits and that spirit will try it's best to wreak havoc in your marriage through an open door. Seducing spirits can enter a marriage through the wrong associations with people even at church. Just because you and your spouse go to church doesn't mean demons and spirits don't go to church as well. Those tend to be the worse that appear to be holy and righteous that can either make or break a marriage with temptations, manipulations, accusations, suspicions and lies. There are many wolves in sheep's clothing that come to church displaying the characteristics of a servant to help the couple's ministry but a heart carrying divisive motives. They can come in the guise of helping the ministry but desire to cause friction in the marriage. Deceptive spirits can fool even the very elect with the enemy who uses any weak vessel to get your marriage in disorder. Marriage doesn't exempt you from demonic spirits and people coming against you or your mate. Some people see you being married as a challenge or contest to see if they can seduce the husband, wife or both. That's why keeping you and your spouse out of compromising positions is vital to not bring a reproach on the marriage. Trusting one another keeps the marriage from being divided by the spirit of discord. God will reveal to you and your spouse what the enemy is scheming towards your family and in your family worship time, this is when you counterattack by canceling every satanic weapon that is formed against your marriage.

Chapter 7

Marriage as Ministry

Marriage is more than just finding your soulmate and living happily ever after. God designed marriage as a ministry exclusive from other ministerial capacities that people are ordained for. The two persons are selected for marriage based on the will of God being established in their life. Not everyone is intended or desires to be married. The single state is not an incomplete status, it is a deceptive thought to think that everyone is destined to be married. This becomes evident in what Paul declared in 1Corinthians 7:7 "For I would that all men were even as I myself. But every man hath his proper gift of God, one after this manner, and another after that." (KJV). In verses 8,9, Paul conveys that "I say therefore to the unmarried and widows, it is good for them if they abide even as I. But if they cannot contain, let them marry: for it is better to marry than to burn. Paul advises those who are in a single state that desire marriage to get married in order to not sin through fornication, lust and premarital sex. Yet, you can't just get married just to have the permission to have permissible sex under the eyes of God, but marriage is a ministry that you must be ready and equipped to handle. Marriage is just like any other ministry or calling like apostles, pastors, teachers, prophets, and evangelists. It is to be taken seriously and not just to have companionship in one's life because you are tired of being lonely on a Friday night, or going to a wedding alone. Marriage is not the magic button that fixes all your emotional and mental issues because you thought having a soulmate will make you stable in your emotions and mind. It is also not to be used to achieve success in life or feel more important being called Mr. and Mrs. The gift of marriage is a gift from God that He grants to those who are ready to take on this next spiritual elevation and level in the Kingdom of God. It is a divine connection between two people under the eyes of God to be fruitful, multiply and have dominion in the earth. Also, godly marriages will also help advance the Kingdom of God and help spread the gospel of Jesus Christ throughout the earth. God doesn't join random people together by arbitrary chance for them to enjoy the carnal things of the world but to do a work for Him as well. Marrying the wrong person can hinder your ministry and getting hitched for fleshly passions isn't ministry either. Both husband and wife need to work together in ministry in unity and desire to see other people whole and complete in God. They both come together with the unique ministries God has given and fused together into a ministry of oneness and unity to help souls grow in the things of God. There is a divine purpose into marrying another soul. The divine purpose of getting married to someone is always in alignment with God's perfect will for their lives and ministry. Even in the act of marriage, you must be devoted, loyal and committed to a person for a lifetime which is a ministry. Then as you both work in the ministry and towards the things of God, both spouses must have a balance between their divine master, ministry and married life. As a spouse, you must devote your time to God, your mate, and your ministry with wisdom by the leading of the Holy Spirit. The Holy Spirit will help you to find balance in your life and not become imbalanced in devoting more time in one area than another. Sometimes we can spend an excessive length of time doing ministry outside of our homes that we forget our first ministry which is with God and our spouses. We need to make sure our spouses spiritual and natural needs are met which enrich the married life. Everything we see manifested in our lives is the result of what we've been cultivating and focusing on in our private lives. You can't preach, teach, pray, and minister effectively to others if you can't do it for yourself and especially for your spouse. Your relationship with your spouse is a direct reflection of your personal relationship with God. Our ministry should reflect our relationship with our spouses. If there's imbalance in the home then you'll see it in the ministry or at church. Now that old saying, "Charity starts at home," is true in every facet of a person's life even in marriage. There must be a balance in marriage and God in which each get equal quality time. You can't neglect your spiritual needs with God nor the needs of your spouse. True ministry requires servitude and sacrifices in your marriage and in ministry. Ministry is just the ability to serve others and spouses must be able to serve one another as well as others in the spirit of meekness and love. You have double power, favor and anointing on your marriage when the two of you function as one vessel of honor and truth. Marriage is an earthly representation of the relationship God has with mankind and how we are to show our devotion to God as we worship Him in spirit and in truth. How you treat God is how you are going to treat your spouse. Your relationship with your spouse should reflect your love for God. Your marriage should not reflect your love for the world and the lust of your flesh. It should show the love of God in its totality and your marriage should enrich this love not subtract or separate you from the love of your

God. Nothing on this earth that includes your marriage should separate you from the love of your God as it is written in the book of Romans 8:39. Marriages should not be a hindrance or stumbling block to your walk with God especially to your ministry. When Ahab married Jezebel in the book of 1st Kings 16:31, he began to serve other idols and gods no longer worshipping the one true living God. He had married a woman who didn't love God and wanted to serve her other gods which doomed the marriage from the beginning. The scripture says Ahab took upon himself to build altars for the idol Baal because he wanted to appease his wife Jezebel. This sent the Kingdom into an uproar with Jezebel attacking and killing God's prophets with Ahab allowing his wife to destroy God's people. This biblical story serves as an example of the consequence of marrying outside of the will of God. Their marriage caused considerable harm, both met an untimely demise and were eternally damned because they didn't desire to worship God but followed other gods.

Even in marriage, the spirit of compromise and idolatry can never have entrance or margin in your life because it will wreak havoc on you and your spouse's lives and others in ministry. Your spouse should continue to follow God and never seek other gods nor compromise their walk with God. If your spouse is beginning to compromise in their spiritual walk, you must pray for them so that they don't get deceived or begin to walk contrary to the principles of God. Marriage is supposed to be rewarding and enhancing in every aspect of your life that will affect generations to come. True and authentic marriages are to leave a legacy of unity and help to inspire other people to desire to have a godly marriage. The right marriage can birth a greater destiny and bring forth greater exploits done in the Kingdom of God to benefit generations to come. Joseph and Mary are a prime example of a marriage that brought forth a destiny that would save mankind and deliver the world from destruction. In the book of Matthew, Mary was visited by an Angel telling her that she was going to birth a son from God and at the time she was engaged to a man named Joseph. Before she got married, she was pregnant by the Holy Ghost who divinely carried Jesus Christ. At first, Joseph was going to get rid of Mary because she became pregnant without being married. Consequently, Joseph was visited by an Angel who shared who she was carrying. As a married couple, you must understand and know what God has put in you and your spouse's life in terms of gifts, talents and anointings to come together to birth a ministry together. Once Joseph and Mary realized the importance of this child, they embraced their responsibility as a married couple who have been given the charge of raising God's son, Jesus on the earth. Joseph was chosen to marry Mary to protect her and be the father to Jesus on the earth. Mary was chosen by God to carry and birth the Savior of the world. Their marriage was crucial to ensuring that Jesus was born safely and securely into the world to carry out His mandate in the earth. Destiny was born by a married couple who were chosen by God to help Jesus grow up into his purpose of winning souls and destroying the works of Satan in the earth. God finds delight in seeing marriages truly flourish and affect the lives of others in a positive manner. Marriage becomes a way of life that should take you deeper in the things of God and desire the more of God. Your spouse can never take the place of God in your life nor make you complete as a person.

Chapter 8 Provider as Mate

As Christians God proves that He alone gives us the power to get wealth, the favor to secure employment and even provide surprise blessings. As we trust God in faith to continually provide both naturally and spiritually as singles or as a married couple. Most importantly in the single state we must learn to trust in Him to supply every need in our lives according to His riches in glory in Christ Jesus as described in Philippians 4:19 (KJV). With that foundation as a single person it will be transferred into a marriage that God is the ultimate source. The belief that getting married is a way of getting a provider in our lives, so they can help pay the bills and we can live more secured financially is erroneous. It is not a stable or good way to enter any marriage covenant with someone based on finances alone even though finances are just as important as praying and fasting in the right context. But if you are trying to get married for financial security, you can remain single and have a roommate or friend help you out in that area. Marriage is a serious commitment and shouldn't be entered into lightly because you're tired or overwhelmed paying for everything by yourself and you now want to live comfortably enjoying the finer things in life. Some people still marry people not necessarily out of love but out of circumstance and how they can help meet their financial obligations. Our mate shouldn't be viewed as the goose that laid the golden egg nor a personal banker. Let's look at how God wants us to see our mate as a provider but not our sole provider. Now the man in the household was designed and created to protect and provide for his family. The woman should work to ensure that her husband is a provider and protector in the family but not rely on him for everything financial or tangible needs. Both man and woman should have their lives based on God being their provider whether they have jobs, businesses or are in full-time ministry. In marriage, both spouses should walk in a level of faith and belief that God is going to take care of them once they have done all they can and trust God for the increase and overflow. Having good credit, practicing the ability to budget and the discipline to save benefits in marriage in handling financial obligations. Even if you marry someone that is wealthy or abundantly supplied, you must be good stewards of your financial blessings. When men don't act as a provider and expect the woman to do it all, that's when you have an imbalance in the marriage and this can cause false burdens to be put on one spouse to take care of the needs of the family. On the other hand, if a woman doesn't provide any financial support to her husband to help meet the financial needs of the household can cause stress, arguments and possible separation that leads to divorce. When you are in full-time ministry, both spouses must believe in faith that God will supply their needs. God will direct you to work a natural job or vision to own a business to bring in other streams of income. In the book of Ruth, we see how the wealthy man was a provider and how the woman was working in the field. Both were working to produce and make things for themselves. God always wants to bless the work of our hands but we have to be working at something in order for Him to bless and increase it whether it's a job, business or personal ministry. Ruth and Naomi went to Judah after losing their husbands. Ruth managed to get an opportunity to get corn out of the fields of the landowner named Boaz. Boaz was a relative to Naomi. He noticed Ruth working in the fields not waiting for a man to provide for her but she was trusting God to be her provider. She eventually found favor with Boaz who let her take as much corn as possible back home to her and Naomi. Later in the book of Ruth, Boaz made Ruth his wife becoming a provider and husband to her blessing her family as well. In that she bore a son that would eventually be the father of King David leading to Jesus Christ being the Son of God through the family lineage. Your mate becomes your provider in a sense of being a confidante, friend and someone you can lean on during troubles, difficulties and struggles that may arise in your marriage. But the true provider in all things must be the divine source of God in marriage. Couples should not become overwhelmed with false burdens and trying to do things in their strength and might. God will take care of His children.

Covenant Agreement For Husband

I _____ (husband) agree to be the leader, provider and protector God destined me to be. I agree to water my wife with the word of God. I agree not to allow any outside influences into our home. I also agree to an open platform for communication and not feel diminished if my wife offers constructive criticism. I agree not to enter any emotional relationships with other women. I also agree to seek outside counsel with a trusted Pastor when my marriage is facing problems I need guidance with. I agree to love, honor, respect and cherish my wife for the rest of my life.

Read aloud to your wife.

_____

Signature

Covenant Agreement For Wife

I _____ (wife) agree to be the helpmeet and helpmate that my husband needs. I also agree not to enter any unhealthy relationship with a man or discuss my marriage or husband in a negative manner. I agree to prayer before communicating tough conversations and filtering everything through the lens of love. I agree not to confront my husband in public or disrespect him to bring public shame. I also agree to love, honor and respect him as the head of our household for the rest of my life.

Read aloud to your husband.

_____

Signature

About the Author

International speaker and television host, Dr. Veynell Warren is the Pastor of Believers International Ministries and founder of Believers International Theological Seminary in Dallas Texas. Dr. Warren has been a successful entrepreneur for 35 years. As President and CEO of Crazy Faith Entertainment, Dr. Warren has been privileged to work with Grammy award winning Gospel Artist and manage several Gospel Artist. "Balancing Between My Marriage and My Mate," is Dr. Warren's unfiltered and unapologetic God inspired interpretation of the biblical design for marriage. The revelation comprised in the book promises to leave readers astounded.

Made in the USA
Columbia, SC
08 November 2023